THE WNBA FINALS

by Tyler Omoth

CAPSTONE PRESS
a capstone imprint

Capstone Captivate is published by Capstone Press, an imprint of Capstone.
1710 Roe Crest Drive
North Mankato, Minnesota 56003.
www.capstonepub.com

Copyright © 2020 Capstone. All rights reserved. No part of this publication may be reproduced in whole or in part, or stored in a retrieval system, or transmitted in any form or by any means, electronic, mechanical, photocopying, recording, or otherwise, without written permission of the publisher.

Library of Congress Cataloging-in-Publication Data is available on the Library of Congress website.
ISBN: 978-1-5435-9193-4 (hardcover)
ISBN: 978-1-4966-5783-1 (paperback)
ISBN: 978-1-5435-9200-9 (eBook PDF)

Summary:
Learn all about the surprising facts, amazing stories, and legendary players found in this book.

Image Credits
Associated Press: Brett Coomer, 24, Elaine Thompson, cover, Jim Mone, 5, Kamil Krzaczynski, 29, Kevork Djansezian, 7; Dreamstime: Danny Raustadt, 9, Doug James, 8, 23 (top), Keeton10, 11; Newscom: Icon SMI/SI/John McDonough, 13, 15, 21, Icon SMI/Richard Clement, 16, MCT/Hyosub Shin, 23 (bottom), Reuters/Rebecca Cook, 17, Reuters/Robert Galbraith, 14, TNS/Aaron Lavinsky, 19, USA Today Sports/Brad Rempel, 26, USA Today Sports/Jennifer Buchanan, 10; Shutterstock: EFKS, 1

Design Elements: Shutterstock

Editorial Credits
Editor: Gena Chester; Designer: Sarah Bennett; Media Researcher: Eric Gohl; Production Specialist: Spencer Rosio

All internet sites appearing in back matter were available and accurate when this book was sent to press.

Printed and bound in China.
PA99

Table of Contents

INTRODUCTION
The Big Game Winner 4

CHAPTER 1
The History 6

CHAPTER 2
Great Teams 12

CHAPTER 3
Hardwood Heroes 20

Glossary 30
Read More 31
Internet Sites 31
Index 32

Glossary terms are **bold** on first use.

INTRODUCTION

The Big Game Winner

The Los Angeles Sparks played the Minnesota Lynx in the last game of the 2016 WNBA Finals. Most fans thought the Sparks would win. But the game was neck-and-neck. With just 3.1 seconds left on the clock, Sparks forward Nneka Ogwumike grabbed a rebound and tried to shoot. Her shot was blocked, but she grabbed the ball again.

Falling backward, she tossed up one more shot. This time she got nothing but net! The Sparks led 77–76. They held on to win the game and the 2016 WNBA Finals.

Fast Fact!

Minnesota Lynx head coach Cheryl Reeves has the most **playoff** wins of any coach in WNBA history. She's tied for the most WNBA championships with four.

Nneka Ogwumike sinks a shot while falling backwards. Her basket was the deciding play in the 2016 Finals.

CHAPTER 1

The History

On April 24, 1996, the board of directors for the National Basketball Association (NBA) voted to create a women's pro basketball **league**. The new league would be called the Women's National Basketball Association (WNBA). The WNBA featured eight teams. The first game tipped off in June of 1997. The New York Liberty faced the Los Angeles Sparks.

That game drew in 14,284 fans. The Liberty defeated the Sparks by a score of 67–57. The regular season was underway. Each team played 28 games.

The Originals

The WNBA started with only eight teams, split into two **conferences**. The Eastern Conference had the Charlotte Sting, Cleveland Rockers, Houston Comets, and New York Liberty. The Los Angeles Sparks, Phoenix Mercury, Sacramento Monarchs, and Utah Starzz made up the Western Conference.

L.A. Sparks center Zheng Haixia (middle) shoots over Rebecca Lobo of the New York Liberty.

7

Once the regular season was complete, the playoffs started. The four teams with the best records competed against each other. After a first round of playoff games, only two teams were left. The Houston Comets beat the New York Liberty in a one-game Finals Championship. It was the start of many wins for the Houston Comets.

Detroit Shock player Katie Smith calls out a play during a regular season game. In 2009, the Shock eventually moved to Dallas, Texas, and are now called the Dallas Wings.

Lynx star Maya Moore attempts a shot. The Mercury went on to win the game and the Western Conference Finals 85–71 in 2014.

Over one million fans went to see WNBA games that first season. The new league was considered a success. It was ready for season number two. For the second season, two more teams entered the league—the Detroit Shock and Washington Mystics.

The WNBA has continued to grow and change. Today, there are 12 teams in the WNBA. They are the Atlanta Dream, Chicago Sky, Connecticut Sun, Indiana Fever, New York Liberty, Washington Mystics, Dallas Wings, Los Angeles Sparks, Las Vegas Aces, Minnesota Lynx, Phoenix Mercury, and Seattle Storm.

Each season, the top four teams from each conference go to the playoffs. There are four rounds of games. In rounds one and two, each team plays just one game. Winning teams move to the next round. Losing teams in the first two rounds are out of the playoffs.

Seattle Storm guard Jewell Lloyd (right) goes for a layup in Game 2 of the 2018 WNBA Finals.

The Dallas Wings pass the ball around the Mercury defense in a 2017 game.

Round three, the Conference Finals, is a best-of-five series. That means the team that wins three games first wins.

The two winning teams from the third round play each other in the WNBA Finals. This is also a best-of-five series. The first team to win three games is named the WNBA Champion for the season.

CHAPTER 2

Great Teams

Houston Comets: 1997–2000

In 1997 through 2000, it looked like the new WNBA league was going to belong to the Houston Comets. Teammates Cynthia Cooper, Cheryl Swoops, and Tina Thompson helped the Comets win the first four WNBA Finals. During those four seasons, the Comets won 114 games and lost only 26. The Comets won every time they reached the WNBA Finals.

The early success of the Houston Comets was not enough to keep the team alive. The team shut down in 2008. A search for new ownership had failed. The Comets were dropped from the WNBA.

The Houston Comets celebrate winning the 2000 WNBA Championship. Cynthia Cooper (14) won the WNBA Championship Most Valuable Player Award for the second time.

Fast Fact!

The Women's Basketball Hall of Fame is in Knoxville, Tennessee. Cynthia Cooper and Tina Thompson were added in 2009 and 2018.

Nikki Teasley of the Sparks and Tari Phillips of the Liberty dive for a loose ball. The Sparks won Game 2 of the 2002 Finals 69–66.

Los Angeles Sparks: 2001–2003

The Los Angeles Sparks picked up where the Comets left off. They play in the Staples Center. That's also where the Los Angeles Lakers play. The Sparks head coach, Michael Cooper, had been a star player for the Lakers.

The Sparks were led by Lisa Leslie. The 6-foot, 5-inch tall center helped them win 28 games in 2001. They lost only four games that season. In the playoffs, they won the Conference Semifinals and WNBA Finals without losing a single game.

In 2002, they did it again. The Sparks won the Championship without losing a single playoff game. In 2003, they made it to the Finals a third time but were defeated by the Detroit Shock.

All-Star player Lisa Leslie shoots a free throw in the 2001 WNBA Finals. Leslie retired from the league in 2009.

Detroit Shock: 2003–2008

The Shock had the WNBA's worst record in 2002. New head coach Bill Laimbeer made big changes to the **roster**. He added Ruth Riley, Cheryl Ford, and Kendra Holland-Corn to the lineup. These players added big talent in scoring and rebounding. From 2003 to 2008, the Detroit Shock were one of the best teams in the WNBA.

In 2003, they defeated the Los Angeles Sparks to win the WNBA Finals. Center Ruth Riley was named the WNBA Finals MVP. They won the Finals again in 2006 and 2008. They made it to the Finals in 2007 but were defeated by the Phoenix Mercury.

The Shock's Swin Cash dribbles up the court during Game 3 of the 2006 WNBA Finals.

Detroit Shock players Plenette Pierson (left) and Cheryl Ford celebrate a made shot by Ford in Game 2 of the 2008 WNBA Finals.

The Shock remained a strong team for several years. They went from one of the WNBA's worst teams to one of the best. A lack of money forced the Shock to move to Tulsa, Oklahoma, in 2010. In 2015, the team moved again. This time they became the Dallas Wings.

Minnesota Lynx: 2011–2017

The Minnesota Lynx entered the WNBA in 1999. It took the team 12 years to make it to the Finals. The 2011 season started one of the strongest WNBA teams ever.

The Lynx won the Finals in 2011 behind the strong play of Seimone Augustus. They weren't done. They won it all in 2013, 2015, and 2017.

WNBA stars like Maya Moore, Sylvia Fowles, and Lindsay Whalen made them a great team year after year. Head coach Cheryl Reeves became the most successful coach in WNBA history.

Fast Fact!

The Lynx and Houston Comets share the record for winning the most WNBA Finals Championships. They each have four.

Lynx guard Seimone Augustus (middle) steals the ball from fallen Sparks forward Nneka Ogwumike. The Lynx have made it to the WNBA Finals six times.

CHAPTER 3

Hardwood Heroes

Cynthia Cooper: Houston Comets

Cynthia Cooper was 34 years old when she played her first WNBA game. Despite her age, she was an immediate star. She led the Houston Comets to four straight WNBA Finals Championships. She was the WNBA Finals MVP each time.

She is the all-time leader in points-per-game in the WNBA. Her average was 21 points-per-game during regular seasons. When it was playoff time, she got even better. After four playoffs, she averaged 23.3 points-per-game.

No one has ever been as consistently good in the playoffs as Cooper. She retired in 2004. Five years later, Cooper was voted into the Women's Basketball Hall of Fame in 2009.

Cynthia Cooper shoots a free throw during Game 2 of the 2000 WNBA Finals. Cooper helped the Comets win several WNBA Championships.

Angel McCoughtry: Atlanta Dream

Angel McCoughtry can do it all. She was the WNBA Rookie of the Year in 2009 and helped Team USA win two gold medals at the Olympics. She's been an All-Star five times. She's a great defender and scorer.

But when the Atlanta Dream go to the playoffs, she really shines. In 2010, McCoughtry set the WNBA record for most points in a playoff game. She scored 42 points in the conference finals game against the New York Liberty. Her team won 105–93.

The next year, she saved her best for Game 2 of the WNBA Finals. She scored 38 points against the Minnesota Lynx. That's the most points by one player ever in a WNBA Finals game.

Fast Fact!

WNBA players usually play **overseas** during their off-season. Playing overseas is a great way for WNBA players to make more money. But without the rest that comes with an off-season, players are more at risk for injury.

Angel McCoughtry (right) drives to the hoop during a game against the Phoenix Mercury.

McCoughtry goes up for a layup in Game 3 of the 2011 WNBA Finals.

Teresa Weatherspoon: New York Liberty

The New York Liberty were facing the Houston Comets in the 1999 WNBA Finals. The Comets held a 2–0 lead in the series. With just 2.4 seconds left to play, the Liberty were trailing by two points. Confetti began to fall onto the court as the Comets fans began to celebrate.

The game wasn't over yet. The Liberty threw a long **inbound pass** in to guard Teresa Weatherspoon. Weatherspoon took two quick dribbles toward the hoop and launched a half-court shot. The ball smacked the backboard and went in for a 3-point shot. The Liberty won the game!

While the Comets won the championship in the next game, Weatherspoon's half-court shot is one of the most memorable moments in WNBA history.

New York Liberty's Teresa Weatherspoon is swarmed by her teammates after making an amazing, buzzer-beating shot from half court. With Weatherspoon's shot, the Liberty took the Comets to a deciding Game 3 in 1999.

Lynx forward Maya Moore dribbles against Sparks defender Odyssey Sims.

Maya Moore: Minnesota Lynx

Minnesota Lynx star Maya Moore is great at proving herself in big moments. In Game 3 of the 2015 WNBA Finals, she made one of the biggest shots in WNBA history.

With just 1.7 seconds left to play, the game was tied 77–77. Teammate Lindsay Whalen threw an inbound pass in to Moore at the top of the 3-point line. Moore faked a shot, then stepped to her right. The defender flew past her. Moore jumped and fired. The ball went through the net perfectly! The shot gave Minnesota the win by a score of 80–77.

Fast Fact!
Maya Moore is a highly decorated athlete. She has been an All-Star six times and won the All-Star MVP three times. She's scored more points in WNBA All-Star games than any other player.

Diana Taurasi: Phoenix Mercury

Phoenix Mercury guard Diana Taurasi likes the number three. She wears jersey number three. She's even the all-time career leader in 3-pointers in the WNBA.

So it's no surprise that her biggest moment came during Game 3 of the 2014 WNBA Finals. The Mercury were winning the series 2–0. The game was tied with just under 15 seconds left to play when Taurasi took a running shot just outside the lane.

Taurasi made the basket and was also fouled by her defender. She made her free throw to make it a 3-point play. The Mercury won the game and the Finals for their third WNBA Championship.

Equal Pay?

The average WNBA player is paid around $79,000 annually. The league limits **salaries** to at most $117,500. In comparison, the starting salary for men in the NBA in 2019 was $582,180. The salary limit for an NBA player was $109 million for the 2019–2020 season. LeBron James made $35.65 million in 2018. That's enough money to pay the salaries of all players in the WNBA for two full seasons.

Mercury guard Diana Taurasi shoots in Game 3 of the 2014 WNBA Finals. In 2015, Taurasi's overseas team in Russia paid her to sit out of the upcoming WNBA season. The move sparked further debate over paying WNBA players a fair salary.

Glossary

conference (KAHN-fuhr-uhns)—a grouping of sports teams that play against each other

defense (di-FENS)—the team that tries to stop points from being scored

inbound pass (in-BOWND PASS)—a pass from outside the playing area into the playing area

league (LEEG)—a group of sports teams that play against each other

overseas (o-vur-SEES)—in or to a country that is not in North America

playoff (PLAY-awf)—a series of games played after the regular season to decide a championship

roster (ROSS-tur)—a list of players on a team

salary (SAL-uh-ree)—money paid on a regular schedule to people doing a job

Read More

Buckley, James Jr. *It's a Numbers Game: Basketball.* Washington, DC: National Geographic Kids, 2020.

Delle Donne, Elena. *My Shot: Balancing It All and Standing Tall.* New York: Simon & Schuster Books for Young Readers, 2018.

Mortensen, Lori. *Maya Moore: Basketball Star.* North Mankato, MN: Capstone Press, 2018.

Internet Sites

Jr. NBA
jr.nba.com

Official Site of the WNBA
www.wnba.com

The Los Angeles Sparks
sparks.wnba.com

Index

Atlanta Dream, 10
    McCoughtry, Angel, 22

Charlotte Sting, 6
Chicago Sky, 10
Cleveland Rockers, 6
Connecticut Sun, 10

Dallas Wings, 10, 17
Detroit Shock, 9, 15, 16, 16–17
    Ford, Cheryl, 16
    Holland-Corn, Kendra, 16
    Laimbeer, Bill, 16
    Riley, Ruth, 16

fans, 9

Houston Comets, 6, 8, 12, 18, 25
    Cooper, Cynthia, 12, 13, 20
    Swoops, Cheryl, 12
    Thompson, Tina, 12, 13

Indiana Fever, 10

Las Vegas Aces, 10
Los Angeles Sparks, 4, 6, 10, 15, 16
    Cooper, Michael, 15
    Leslie, Lisa, 15
    Ogwumike, Nneka, 4

Minnesota Lynx, 4, 10, 18, 22
    Augustus, Seimone, 18
    Fowles, Sylvia, 18
    Moore, Maya, 18, 27
    Reeves, Cheryl, 4, 18
    Whalen, Lindsay, 18, 27
money, 22, 28

National Basketball Association (NBA), 6
New York Liberty, 6, 8, 10, 22, 25
    Weatherspoon, Teresa, 25

off-season, 22
Olympics, 22

Phoenix Mercury, 6, 10, 16, 28
    Taurasi, Diana, 28
playoffs, 8, 10, 15, 20, 22

records, 8

Sacramento Monarchs, 6
Seattle Storm, 10
Staples Center, 15

Utah Starzz, 6

Washington Mystics, 9, 10
Women's Basketball Hall of Fame, 13, 20